Selected Poems-V

Selected Poems - V

Rabindranath Tagore

Rupa & Co

Concept & Typeset coypyright © Rupa & Co 2002

Published 2002 by
Rupa & Co
7/16, Ansari Road, Daryaganj
New Delhi 110 002

Offices at:
15 Bankim Chatterjee Street, Kolkata 700 073
135 South Malaka, Allahabad 211 001
PG Solanki Path, Lamington Road, Mumbai 400 007
36, Kutty Street, Nungambakkam, Chennai 600 034
Surya Shree, B-6, New 66, Shankara Park,
Basavangudi, Bangalore 560 004
3-5-612, Himayat Nagar, Hyderabad 500 029

Design & Typeset by
Arrt Creations
45 Nehru Apts, Kalkaji
New Delhi 110 019

Printed in India by
Gopsons Papers Ltd
A-14, Sector 60, Noida - 201 301

previous page: Rabindranath Tagore.

Contents

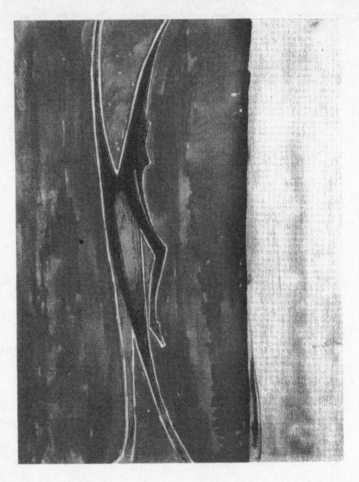

Ink on paper. Signed 'Sri Rabindra' in Bengali.18.8 X 24.7 cm

Gitanjali

❧

I WAS NOT aware of the moment when I first crossed
the threshold of this life.

What was the power that made me open out into this
vast mystery like a bud in the forest at midnight!

When in the morning I looked upon the light I felt in
a moment that I was no stranger in this world, that
the inscrutable without name and form had taken
me in its arms in the form of my own mother.

Even so, in death the same unknown will appear as
ever known to me. And because I love this life, I
know I shall love death as well.

The child cries out when from the right breast the
mother takes it away, in the very next moment to
find in the left one its consolation.

~

WHEN I GO from hence let this be my parting word,
that what I have seen is unsurpassable.
I have tasted of the hidden honey of this lotus that
expands on the ocean of light, and thus am I
blessed—let this be my parting word.
In this playhouse of infinite forms I have had my play
and here have I caught sight of him that is
formless.
My whole body and my limbs have thrilled with his
touch who is beyond touch; and if the end comes
here, let it come—let this be my parting word.

I DIVE DOWN into the depth of the ocean of forms,

hoping to gain the perfect pearl of the formless.

No more sailing from harbour to harbour with this my

weather-beaten boat. The days are long passed

when my sport was to be tossed on waves.

And now I am eager to die into the deathless.

Into the audience hall by the fathomless abyss where

swells up the music of toneless strings I shall take

this harp of my life.

I shall tune it to the notes of for ever, and, when it has

sobbed out its last utterance, lay down my silent

harp at the feet of the silent.

IN ONE salutation to thee, my God, let all my senses
spread out and touch this world at thy feet.

Like a rain-cloud of July hung low with its burden of
unshed showers let all my mind bend down at thy
door in one salutation to thee.

Let all my songs, gather together their diverse strains
into a single current and flow to a sea of silence in
one salutation to thee.

Like a flock of homesick cranes flying night and day
back to their mountain nests let all my life take its
voyage to its eternal home in one salutation to
thee.

The Crescent Moon

THE WICKED POSTMAN

WHY DO YOU sit there on the floor so quiet and silent,
   tell me mother dear?

The rain is coming in through the open window,
   making you all wet, and you don't mind it.

Do you hear the going striking four? It is time for my
   brother to come home from school.

What has happened to you that look so strange?

Haven't you got a letter from father to-day?

I saw the postman bringing letters in his bag for almost
   everybody in the town.

Only, father's letters he keeps to read himself. I am
   sure the postman is a wicked man.

But don't be unhappy about that, mother dear.

To-morrow is market day in the next village. You ask
    your maid to buy some pens and papers.

I myself will write all father's letters; you will not find a
    single mistake.

I shall write from A right up to K.

But, mother, why do you smile?

You don't believe that I can write as nicely as father
    does!

But I shall rule my paper carefully, and write all the
    letters beautifully big.

When I finish my writing, do you think I shall be so
    foolish as father and drop it into the horrid
    postman's bag?

I shall bring it to you myself without waiting, and letter
    by letter help you to my writing.

I know the postman does not like to give you the really
    nice letters.

THE HERO

MOTHER, LET us imagine we are travelling, and passing
  through a strange and dangerous country.

You are riding in a palanquin and I am trotting by you
  on a red horse.

It is evening and the sun goes down. The waste of
  Joradighi lies wan and grey before us. The land is
  desolate and barren.

You are frightened and thinking—'I know not where
  we have come to.'

I say to you, 'Mother, do not be afraid.'

The meadow is prickly with spiky grass, and through it
  runs a narrow broken path.

There are no cattle to be seen in the wide field; they
  have gone to their village stalls.

It grows dark and dim on the land and sky, and we
    cannot tell where we are going.

Suddenly you call me and ask me in a whisper, 'What
    light is that near the bank?'

Just then there bursts out a fearful yell, and figures
    come running towards us.

You sit crouched in your palanquin and repeat the
    names of the gods in prayer.

The bearers, shaking in terror, hide themselves in the
    thorny bush.

I shout to you, 'Don't be afraid, mother, I am here.'

With long sticks in their hands and hair all wild about
    their heads, they come nearer and nearer.

I shout, 'Have a care! you villains! One step more and
    you are dead men.'

They give another terrible yell and rush forward.

You clutch my hand and say, 'Dear boy, for heaven's
sake, keep away from them.'

I say, 'Mother, just you watch me.'

Then I spur my horse for a wild gallop, and my sword
and buckler clash against each other.

The fight becomes so fearful, mother, that it would
give you a cold shudder could you see it from your
palanquin.

Many of them fly, and a great number are cut to
pieces.

I know you are thinking, sitting all by yourself, that
your boy must be dead by this time.

But I come to you all stained with blood, and say,
'Mother, the fight is over now.'

You come out and kiss me, pressing me to your heart,
    and you say to yourself.
'I don't know what I should do if I hadn't my boy to
    escort me.'
A thousand useless things happen day after day, and
    why couldn't such a thing come true by chance?
It would be like a story in a book.
My brother would say, 'Is it possible? I always thought
    he was so delicate!'
Our village people would all say in amazement, 'Was it
    not lucky that the boy was with his mother?'

THE LAST BARGAIN

'COME AND HIRE ME,' I cried, while in the morning I was
    walking on the stone-paved road.
Sword in hand, the King came in his chariot.
He held my hand and said, 'I will hire you with my
    power.'
But his power counted for nought, and he went away
    in his chariot.

In the heat of the midday the houses stood with shut
    doors.
I wandered along the crooked lane.
An old man came out with his bag of gold.
He pondered and said, 'I will hire you with my money.'
He weighed his coins one by one, but I turned away.

It was evening. The garden hedge was all aflower.

The fair maid came out and said, 'I will hire you with a
smile.'

Her smile paled and melted into tears, and she went
back alone into the dark.

The sun glistened on the sand, and the sea waves
broke waywardly.

A child sat playing with shells.

He raised his head and seemed to know me, and said,
'I hire you with nothing.'

From thenceforward that bargain struck in child's play
made me a free man.

Fruit Gathering

~

To the birds you gave songs, the birds gave you songs
    in return.
You gave me only voice, yet asked for more, and I sing.

You made your winds light and they are fleet in their
    service. You burdened my hands that I myself may
    lighten them, and at last, gain unburdened
    freedom for your service.
You created your Earth filling its shadows with
    fragments of light.
There you paused; you left me empty-handed in the
    dust to create your heaven.
To all things else you give; from me you ask.

The harvest of my life ripens in the sun and the
shower till I reap more than you sowed, gladdening
your heart, O Master of the golden granary.

~

LET ME NOT pray to be sheltered from dangers but to be
fearless in facing them.

Let me not beg for the stilling of my pain but for the
heart to conquer it.

Let me not look for allies in life's battlefield but to my
own strength.

Let me not crave in anxious fear to be saved but hope
for the patience to win my freedom.

Grant me that I may not be a coward, feeling your
mercy in my success alone; but let me find the
grasp of your hand in my failure.

❧

I WILL UTTER your name, sitting alone among the
    shadows of my silent thoughts.

I will utter it without words, I will utter it without
    purpose.

For I am like a child that calls its mother an hundred
    times, glad that it can say 'Mother.'

❧

WHEN THE world sleeps I come to your door.

The stars are silent, and I am afraid to sing.

I wait and watch, till your shadow passes by the
    balcony of night and I return with a full heart.

Then in the morning I sing by the roadside;

The flowers in the hedge give me answer and the

    morning air listens,

The travellers suddenly stop and look in my face,

    thinking I have called them by their names.

Crossing

❧

MY EYES HAVE lost their sleep in watching; yet if I do
not meet thee still it is sweet to watch.

My heart sits in the shadow of the rains waiting for thy
love; if she is deprived still it is sweet to hope.

They walk away in their different paths leaving me
behind; if I am alone still it is sweet to listen for
thy footsteps.

The wistful face of the earth weaving its autumn mists
wakens longing in my heart; if it is in vain still it is
sweet to feel the pain of longing.

HOLD THY FAITH firm, my heart, the day will dawn.

The seed of promise is deep in the soil, it will sprout.

Sleep, like a bud, will open its heart to the light, and
the silence will find its voice.

The day is near when thy burden will become thy gift,
and thy sufferings will light up thy path.

Collected Poems & Plays of Rabindranath Tagore

∿

FILL YOUR EYES with the colours that ripple

on beauty's stream,

vain is your struggle to clutch them.

That which you chase with your desire is a

shadow,

that which thrills your life-chords is music.

The wine they drink at the assembly of gods

has no body, no measure.

It is in rushing brooks,

in flowering trees,

in the smile that dances at the corner of dark eyes.

Enjoy it in freedom.

THOU ART a glimmer of gold from the dawn on my life's

shore,

a dew-drop on the first white flower of autumn.

Thou art a rainbow from the distant sky

bending o'er dust,

a dream of the crescent moon

touched with a white cloud,

thou art a secret of paradise

revealed by chance to the earth.

Thou art my poet's vision,

appearing from the days

of my forgotten birth,

thou art the word that is never for utterance,

a freedom that comes in the form of a bondage,

for thou openest the door for me

to the beauty of a living light.

THE WORLD today is wild the delirium of hatred,

the conflicts are cruel and unceasing in anguish,

crooked are its paths, tangled its bonds of greed.

All creatures are crying for a new birth of thine,

O Thou of boundless life,

save them, rouse thine eternal voice of hope,

Let Love's lotus with its inexhaustible of honey

open its petals in thy light.

O Serene, O Free,

in thine immeasurable mercy and goodness

wipe away all dark stains from the heart of this

earth.

Thou giver of immortal gifts

    give us the power of renunciation

    and claim from us our pride.

    In the splendour of a new sunrise of wisdom

    let the blind gain their sight

    and let life come to the souls that are dead.

O Serene, O Free,

    in thine immeasurable mercy and goodness

    wipe away all dark stains from the heart of this

    earth.

Man's heart is anguished with the fever of unrest,

    with the poison of self-seeking,

    with a thirst that knows no end.

    Countries far and wide flaunt on their foreheads

    the blood-red mark of hatred.

Touch them with thy right hand,

make them one in spirit,

bring harmony into their life,

bring rhythm of beauty.

O Serene, O Free,

in thine immeasurable mercy and goodness

wipe away all dark stains from the heart of this

earth.

❧

WE TWO LAY sunk in the dusk of dreams;

the time of awakening has come

waiting for the last word from you.

Turn your face to me

and with a tear-dimmed glance

make the sorrow of parting
ever beautiful.

The morning will appear with its early star
on the far-distant sky of loneliness.
The pain of this farewell night has been captured
in my *vina*-strings,
the lost glory of love will remain woven in my
visions.
Open with your own hands the door
towards final separation.

❧

ONCE AGAIN I wake up when the night has waned,
when the world opens all its petals once more,
and this is an endless wonder.

Vast islands have sunk in the abyss unnamed,

stars, have been beggared of the last flicker of their
light,

countless epochs have lost all their ladings.

World-conquerors have vanished into the shadow
of a name

behind dim legends,

great nations raised their towers of triumph

as a mere offering to the unappeasable hunger of
the dust.

Among this dissolving crowd of the discarded

my forehead receives the consecration of light,

and this is an endless wonder.

I stand for another day with the Himalayas,

with constellations of stars.

I am here where in the surging sea-waves

the infuriate dance of the Terrible

is rhythmed with his boisterous laughter.

The centuries on which have flashed up and
foundered

kingly crowns like bubbles

have left their signature on the bark of this aged
tree,

where I am allowed to sit under its ancient shade

for one more day,

and this is an endless wonder.

❧

I NEGLECTED to appraise your worth

being blindly sure of my possession.

The days followed each other and the nights

carrying your offerings to my feet.

I looked at them through the corner of my eyes

as they were being sent to my storehouse.
April's honeysuckles added their scent to your
gifts,
the full moon of the autumn night
touched them with its glimmer.

Often your poured the flood of your dark tresses upon my
lap
and your eyes swam with tears while you said:
My tribute to you, my king, is pitifully meagre;
I have failed to give you more, not having any more
to give.

The days follow each other and the nights
but you are no longer here today.
I come to open at last my storehouse,
and take up the chain of the jewels,

that came from your hands on my neck.

My pride that remained indifferent

kisses the dust where you left your footprints.

Today I gain you truly

for with my sorrow I have paid the price of your

love.

∾

IN THAT EARLY dusk of a distracted age,

When God in scorn of his own workmanship

violently shook his head at his primitive efforts,

an impatient wave snatched you away, Africa,

from the bosom of the East,

and kept you brooding in a dense enclosure of

niggardly light,

guarded by giant trees.

There you slowly stored

the baffling mysteries of the wilderness

in the dark cellars of your profound privacy,

conned the signals of land and water difficult to

read;

and the secret magic of Nature invoked in your

mind

magic rites from beyond the boundaries of

consciousness.

You donned the disguise of deformity to mock the

terrible,

and in a mimicry of a sublime ferocity

made yourself fearful to conquer fear.

You are hidden, alas, under a black veil,

which obscures your human dignity

to the darkened vision of contempt.

With man-traps stole upon you those hunters

whose fierceness was keener than the fangs of your
wolves,

whose pride was blinder than your lightless forests.

The savage greed of the civilised stripped naked its
unashamed inhumanity.

You wept and your cry was smothered,

your forest trails became muddy with tears and
blood,

while the nailed boots of the robbers

left their indelible prints

along the history of your indignity.

And all the time across the sea,

church bells were ringing in their towns and
villages,

the children were lulled in mothers' arms,

and poets sang hymns to Beauty.

Today when on the western horizon

    the sunset sky is stifled with dust-storm,

    when the beast, creeping out of its dark den,

    proclaims the death of the day with ghastly howls,

    come, you poet of the fatal hour,

    stand at that ravished woman's door,

    ask for her forgiveness,

    and let that be the last great word

    in the midst of the delirium of a diseased

    Continent.

∼

THE WAR drums are sounded.

    Men force their features into frightfulness and

    gnash their teeth;

    and before they rush out to gather raw human

    flesh for death's larder,

they march to the temple of Buddha, the
compassionate,
to claim his blessings,
while loud beats the drum rat-a-tat
and earth trembles.

They pray for success;
for they must raise weeping and wailing
in their wake, sever ties of love,
plant flags on the ashes of desolated homes,
devastate the centres of culture
and shrines of beauty,
mark red with blood their trail
across green meadows and populous markets,
and so they march tot he temple of Buddha, the
compassionate,
to claim his blessings,

while loud beats the drum rat-a-tat

and earth trembles.

They will punctuate each thousand of the maimed and
  killed
  with the trumpeting of their triumph,
  arouse demon's mirth at the sight
  of the limbs torn bleeding from women and
  children;
  and they pray that they may befog minds with
  untruths
  and poison God's sweet air of breath,
  and therefore they march to the temple of Buddha,
  the compassionate,
  to claim his blessings,
  while loud beats the drum rat-a-tat
  and earth trembles.

MY BIRTHDAY!

With Death's passport in hand

it has emerged from its dive into the chasm of
nothingness

to breathe a while on the outskirts of existence.

From the worn-out chain have dropped the beads

of the past years

and with this newest birthday

begins the counting of the days of a new-born life.

The welcome offered today to me,

a passer-by,

who tries to con the signal of the morning of an

unknown star

beckoning him towards an uncharted voyage,

is shared equally by his birthday

and the time of his death,

who mingle their lights like those of the morning

star

and of the waning moon.

And I shall sing the same chant to both,

to death and to life.

Grant me, Mother Earth,

that my life's mirage born of burning thirst

may recede in the farthest horizon

and my unclean beggar's bowl empty into the dust

its accumulated defilements;

and as I start my crossing to the unrevealed shore

let me never look back with longing

on the last leavings of the feast of life.

Now when in this sleep-laden dusk of the day's end

the meaning is lost of the keen-bladed hunger

with which you had goaded me to drag life's

chariot

you begin to withdraw your gifts from me one by
one.

Slight has grown your need of me

and slight have you made my use

and set on my forehead the stamp of the discarded.

I feel it all and yet I know,

all this contumely of yours

will not reduce my worth to nought.

Cripple me, if you will,

shut out all light from my eyes,

shroud me in the shadow of infirmity,

yet in the dilapidated temple of my being

the ancient god will remain enthroned.

Work your havoc and pile up the wreck,

yet in the midst of this ruin

the luminous spot of inward joy

will burn bright as ever.

For it was fed day after day on the heavenly wine

which the gods pour on earth through every sight

and sound.

I had loved them all

and sung of that love.

That love has lifted me above your bounds,

the love that shall abide, even though its words

grow feeble,

defaced by constant use.

On this love of mine have traced their autographs

the pollen of the mango-blossom,

and the dew-cooled fragrance of the *sephalika*

the twitterings of the *doels* in early dawn

and the rapturous touch of the beloved.

When I take my leave of you, O Earth,

take back from me, carefully reckoning,

all that you had vouchsafed to me,

the outfit and provision for a life's sojourn.

Yet never think that I hold your gifts but slight.

Ever grateful I am to this clay-cast mould

through which I have had my introduction to the

Formless.

Whenever I have approached your doors

with the mind free from all coveting,

I have been made welcome to your heart.

I know your gifts are not for the greedy,

that you withhold the nectar hidden in your

earthen pot

from the ravenous lips of those that hunger

obscenely.

You are waiting, O Earth, with your immortal gifts,

to welcome the wayfarer who treads the arduous
path of detachment.

The gluttons who lust for flesh,
the traffickers in festering carrion,
have banded today in their orgies of violence, day
and night.
Yet mockery tempts my smile, as of old,
at the pompous folly of the learned,
at the tyranny of the beggarly rich,
at the hideous make-up of the showy,
at the blasphemy that lampoons the divine in Man.

Enough of this. The bell tolls the last hour at your
porch,
and my heart responds to the creaking of the
opening gates of farewell.

In this deepening gloom of the twilight,

I will gather what flickering flames remain to light

my fading consciousness,

to offer my last worship to you, O Earth,

under the gaze of the Seven Rishis.

And the incense of my last silent song will float

round you.

Behind me will remain the *nagkeshar* plant

that has yet to flowers,

the anguished heart of this shore

yearning in vain for a ferry across,

and love's self-reproach at its tired memory

vanishing behind the screen of daily task.

SHE IS THE SPIRIT of an Autumn evening,

> robed in the gleams of the vanished sunset,

> carrying the promise of the immense peace of the
> star,

> guiding with her speechless ministry

> the languid steps of the long lingering hours of the
> reluctant night

> into the neighbourhood of the morning star.

> Her tresses touched by the gentle breeze of the
> dawn,

> that smell of the morning worship,

> her sad and sweet face of the day's end

> becomes radiant with the blessedness of the
> morning light.

BLESSINGS HAVE I won in this life

of the Beautiful.

In the vessel of man's affection I taste His own

divine nectar.

Sorrow, hard to bear,

has shown me the unhurt, unconquered soul.

On the day when I felt death's impending shadow,

fear's defeat has not been mine.

The great ones of the Earth

have not deprived me of their touch,

their undying words have I stored in my heart.

Grace I had from the god of life:

this memory let me leave

in grateful words.

One Hundred
Poems of Kabir

❧

I. 79. *tīrath men to sab pānī hai*

THERE IS nothing but water at the holy bathing places;
   and I know that they are useless, for I have bathed
   in them.

The images are all lifeless, they cannot speak; I know,
   for I have cried aloud to them.

The Purana and the Koran are mere words; lifting up
   the curtain, I have seen.

Kabir gives utterance to the words of experience; and
   he knows very well that all other things are
   untrue.

I. 82. *pānī vic mīn piyāsī*

I LAUGH WHEN I hear that the fish in the water is
thirsty:

You do not see that the Real is in your home, and you
wander from forest to forest listlessly!

Here is the truth! Go where you will, to Benares or to
Mathura; if you do not find your soul, the world is
unreal to you.

I. 107. *calat mansā acal kīnhī*

I HAVE STILLED my restless mind, and my heart is
radiant: for in That-ness I have seen beyond

That-ness, in company I have seen the Comrade
    Himself.
Living in bondage, I have set myself free: I have broken
    away from the clutch of all narrowness.
Kabir says: 'I have attained the unattainable, and my
    heart is coloured with the colour of love.'

❦

I. 105. *jo dīsai, so to hai nāhīn*

THAT WHICH you see is not: and for that which is, you
    have no words.
Unless you see, you believe not: what is told you you
    cannot accept.
He who is discerning knows by the word; and the
    ignorant stands gaping.

Some contemplate the Formless, and others meditate
on form: but the wise man knows that Brahma is
beyond both.

That beauty of His is not seen of the eye: that metre of
His is not heard of the ear.

Kabir says: 'He who has found both love and
renunciation never descends to death.'

❧

I. 130. *sāīṇ bin dard kareje hoy*

WHEN I AM parted from my Beloved, my heart is full of
misery: I have no comfort in the day, I have no
sleep in the night. To whom shall I tell my sorrow?

The night is dark; the hours slip by. Because my Lord
is absent, I start up and tremble with fear.

Kabir says: 'Listen, my friend! there is no other
satisfaction, save in the encounter with the
Beloved.'

∾

I. 20. *man na rangāye*

THE YOGI dyes his garments, instead of dyeing his mind
in the colours of love:
He sits within the temple of the Lord, leaving Brahma
to worship a stone.
He pierces holes in his ears, he has a great bear and
matted locks, he looks like a goat:
He goes forth into the wilderness, killing all his desires,
and turns himself into an eunuch:

He shaves his dead and dyes his garments; he reads the
Gita and becomes a mighty talker.

Kabir says: 'You are going to the doors of death, bound
hand and foot!'

∾

III. 102. *ham se rahā na jāy*

I HEAR THE melody of His flute, and I cannot contain
myself:

The flower blooms, though it is not spring; and already
the bee has received its invitation.

The sky roars and the lightning flashes, the waves arise
in my heart,

The rain falls; and my heart longs for my Lord.

Where the rhythm of the world rises and falls, thither

    my heart has reached:

There the hidden banners are fluttering in the air.

Kabir says: 'My heart is dying, though it lives.'

✴

III. 26. *tor hīrā hirāilwā kīcaḍ men*

THE JEWEL IS lost in the mud, and all are seeking for it;

Some look for it in the east, and some in the west;

    some in the water and some amongst stones.

But the servant Kabir has appraised it at its true value,

    and has wrapped it with care in the end of the

    mantle of his heart.

III. 30. *are dil, prem nagar kā ant na pāyā*

O MY HEART! you have not known all the secrets of
this city of love; in ignorance you came, and in
ignorance you return.

O my friend, what have you done with this life? You
have taken on your head the burden heavy with
stones, and who is to lighten it for you?

Your Friend stands on the other shore, but you never
think in your mind how you may meet with Him:

The boat is broken, and yet you sit ever upon the
bank; and thus you are beaten to no purpose by
the waves.

The servant Kabir asks you to consider; who is there
that shall befriend you at the last?

You are alone, you have no companion: you will suffer

the consequences of your own deeds.

❧

III. 66. *nā maiṉ dharmī nahīṉ adharmī*

I AM NEITHER pious nor ungodly,

I live neither by law nor by sense,

I am neither a speaker nor hearer,

I am neither a servant nor master,

I am neither bond nor free,

I am neither detached nor attached.

I am far from none: I am near to none.

I shall go neither to hell nor to heaven.

I do all works; yet I am apart from all works.

Few comprehend my meaning: he who can

comprehend, it, he sits unmoved.

Kabir seeks neither to establish nor to destroy.

❧

III. 84. *jhī jhī jantar bājai*

THE HARP gives forth murmurous music; and the dance

goes on without hands and feet.

It is played without fingers, it is heard without ears: for

He is the ear, and He is the listener.

The gate is locked, but within there is fragrance: and

there the meeting is seen of none.

The wise shall understand it.

Stray Birds

~

MEN ARE cruel, but Man is kind.

~

OUR NAMES are the light that glows on the sea waves at
night and then dies without leaving its signature.

~

MAN IS worse than an animal when he is an animal.

LET MY thoughts come to you, when I am gone, like the afterglow of sunset at the margin of starry silence.

∿

WE LIVE IN this world when we love it.

Fireflies

❧

I MISS THE meaning of my own part

    in the play of life

    because I know not of the parts

    that others play.

❧

THE UNSEEN dark plays on his flute

    and the rhythm of light

    eddies into stars and suns,

    into thoughts and dreams.

WHEN THE voice of the Silent touches my words
I know him and therefore I know myself.

❦

WHEN DEATH comes and whispers to me
'Thy days are ended,'
let me say to him, 'I have lived in love
and not in mere time.'
He will ask 'Will thy songs remains?'
I shall say 'I know not, but this I know
that often when I sang if found my eternity.'